WHAT'S THE MATTER WITH CHRISTMAS?

A Christmas Play In Three Acts

BY PHYLLIS FUTER

**Music By Phyllis Futer
And Lorraine Gernert**

C.S.S. Publishing Co., Inc.
Lima, Ohio

WHAT'S THE MATTER WITH CHRISTMAS?

9252 / ISBN 1-55673-459-X

PRINTED IN U.S.A.

To the children of Leola
United Methodist Church,
our inspiration
And the Christ Child,
our reason

Order Of Worship

*Opening Hymn: "O Come All Ye Faithful"

Responsive Reading

Scripture: Luke 2:1-20

*Hymn: "The Friendly Beasts"

Prayer

*Hymn: "Hark! The Herald Angels Sing"

Offering

*Doxology

*Hymn: "There's A Song In The Air"

Play: "What's The Matter With Christmas?"

*Benediction

*Congregation standing

Characters
Older boy — Willie
Older girl — Becky
Older girl — Lauren
Teenager — Rappin' Jack
Smaller children — Carol, Joey, Jaime, Valerie, Davey, Cheryl,
    Connie, Marty, Gracie, Denise
Salvation Army woman
Mr. Anderson

Performance Time: 35-45 minutes

5

What's The Matter With Christmas?

ACT 1

Willie, Becky and Lauren are sitting on the church steps after Christmas Eve rehearsal. Other children are leaving, excited. Person in charge calls goodbye to the children.

Lauren: I think practice went pretty well today.

Becky: Yeah, even though Connie kept singing off key and Gracie kept having to go to the bathroom.

Lauren: And Davey kept falling off the stage. *(The girls giggle, then look at Willie, who seems to be troubled.)*

Lauren: Willie, what's with you?

Becky: How come you're so quiet today? Don't you know it's only a week until Christmas? If you're not excited now, there's not much hope for you.

Willie: Ah, I don't know . . . something doesn't seem right.

Lauren: Hey, you're serious. What's wrong? What do you mean?

Willie: It's all this hype about Christmas. Everyone is busy doing all kinds of things. Sometimes I feel like I'm in the way at home. And all the kids talk about is what they're going to get.

Lauren: Yeah, and everyone tries to top what someone else is getting.

Becky: Me? I'd like to get a telephone in my room, maybe even my own line and . . .

Lauren: Becky!

Willie: See what I mean? Things, things, things. It just doesn't feel right.

Becky: Hey, I was only kidding. I don't need my own line. I'd be happy with just the phone.

Lauren: Becky! You're not helping Willie one bit.

Willie: It's, it's just that . . . *(Song) What's The Matter With Christmas? (see page A)*

Willie	Everyone is in a hurry Frantic, rushing, worry, worry
Lauren	Driving to the mall and shopping Wrapping presents till they're dropping
Willie	Baking cookies, decorating Looking at the bills and fainting
Lauren	Buying red and silver balls Pushing, shoving in the malls

8

Becky	Now I know what I have missed I didn't put clothing on my list! *(Lauren and Willie moan)*
Willie	Why is it everywhere we turn At this time of year, There's always one more thing to do As Christmas Day draws near?
Willie & **Lauren**	What's the matter with Christmas? Is it something I just don't see? What's the matter with Christmas? What's the matter with me?
Lauren	With grownups racing all around Pulling out their hair They're all uptight and sometimes yell Then kids think they don't care.
Lauren **& Willie**	What's the matter with Christmas? Is it something I just don't see? What's the matter with Christmas? What's the matter with me?

Becky: Boy, you two are depressing!

Willie: I don't mean to be. I just don't . . .

Lauren: You don't see Jesus in it!

Willie: That's it! I don't understand what all this has to do with Jesus. Or God. I mean, why do we do all this?

Becky: All what?

Lauren: The gifts. The wrapping, the shopping, the spending, the commercials.

Becky: If it weren't for commercials, how would we know what we want?

9

Willie: It's hopeless. *(Becky is perplexed)* Oh well, I gotta get home.

Lauren: Me, too. Coming Becky?

Becky: Go on. I have to wait for Gracie. Mr. Anderson is going over what she missed while she was in the bathroom.

(Lauren and Willie leave)

Becky: I don't see what they're so upset about. Christmas is plain to me. *(Song)* ***It's Clear To Me*** *(see page B)*

> **Becky**   I don't see a problem here,
> Things to me are very clear
> Christmas is a wonderful time
> Full of gifts — mostly mine!
>
> I like gum drops, candy canes
> Getting gifts, exchanging names
> It makes me happy, can't they see
> God would want this all for me . . .
> Wouldn't he? *(spoken)*

(Gracie comes running out)

Gracie: Becky, oh, Becky! Guess what I did?

Becky: What?

Gracie: I found Jesus! I found Jesus!

(Mr. Anderson comes out, smiling)

Becky: I didn't know he was lost!

Mr. Anderson: Ah, but he was! Gracie was helping me set up the nativity scene on the altar when we saw that Baby Jesus was missing. We hunted all over the place. We decided to go through the box he was stored in again. We looked carefully through all the old wrappings, piece by piece, till I thought it was no use. But Gracie told me to keep looking.

Gracie: I said, keep looking for Jesus, Mr. Anderson. We can't have Christmas without Jesus!

Mr. Anderson: We looked some more, then finally, down in the corner of the box, there he was. I don't know how I missed him. I must have looked there before, but I guess I couldn't see him for all the other stuff that was in the way.

Gracie: Now we can have Christmas. We found Jesus!

Becky: Hmmm . . . That's great, Gracie. Now let's get home before you have to go to the bathroom again.

(They exit as Mr. Anderson watches.)

ACT II

Scene I — (takes place in the home of one of the children. It's a small Christmas party for the children who are in the Christmas Eve program.)

(All the children and Mr. Anderson)

Valerie: Carol, this was nice of your parents to have a party for us kids. I just love parties!

Carol: I was surprised, too. Usually my mom and dad are bonkers at Christmas time.

Valerie: Mine, too. Mom stays up late baking cookies she doesn't want to eat, and getting cards ready to mail. She says she hates doing cards. I asked her why she does them.

Connie: What did she say, Valerie?

Valerie: She said people expect it. I thought that was a dumb reason, but I didn't say anything.

Connie: Yeah, adults don't like it when kids think their reasons are dumb.

Carol: My parents are different this Christmas. They've actually asked me what are some things I'd like to do this year. That's why I could have this party.

Denise: Hey, you guys! Mr. Anderson wants us to practice our songs.

Mr. Anderson: Okay kids, let's gather round the piano. I thought it would be a good idea to practice our Christmas songs. Let's do "Away In A Manger" first. *(Children sing)*

Joey: Now, let's sing "Silent Night." *(One verse)*

Davey: Let's sing "Happy Birthday" to Jesus! *(Joyfully)*

Mr. Anderson: *(As children break up in their small groups, Lauren, Becky and Willie in one, Connie and Marty near Mr. Anderson.)* That was great, kids. God is pleased to hear your voices celebrating the birth of Jesus.

Marty: *(tugging on Mr. Anderson's pants)* Mr. Anderson! Could you please talk to my brother?

Mr. Anderson: What's wrong with Willie?

Marty: That's what I want you to find out. It's Christmas soon and he doesn't even seem like he cares!

Connie: Doesn't he know how Christmas made everyone happy? Doesn't he know how glad they were Jesus came?

(Song) A Great Big Happy (see page C) (by smaller children — everyone but Lauren, Becky and Willie)

Long ago in Bethlehem
Jesus Christ was born
It was such a happy time
That first Christmas morn.

God felt a great big happy
Too much to keep inside
God felt a great big happy
A love he could not hide.

Angels started songs of praise
They were so filled with joy
They could not keep the good news quiet
About this little boy.

God felt a great big happy
Too much to keep inside
God felt a great big happy
A love he could not hide.

Shepherds ran to see the baby
Walking was too slow
Mary's face was one big smile
She loved her Jesus so!

God felt a great big happy
Too much to keep inside
God felt a great big happy
A love he could not hide.

(Children break up, Mr. Anderson walks over to Becky, Willie and Lauren.)

Becky: Hey, Mr. Anderson, why don't you come sit with us?

Mr. Anderson: Thank you, I will. What's going on over here? You three don't seem very happy tonight.

Becky: It's not me. It's these two.

Mr. Anderson: What's wrong?

Lauren: We're mixed up, I guess. You know how it is when you get older.

Mr. Anderson: Why don't you tell me?

Willie: For some reason, we're not in the Christmas spirit. Everyone is busy with all the preparations for the big day, and for what? You get up early, tear into the presents, and boom! It's over even before Christmas Day is!

Lauren: Yeah, and then you feel all empty and depressed.

Becky: Especially if you didn't get what you wanted and have to pretend you like what you did get.

Lauren and Willie: Becky!

Mr. Anderson: Becky is being honest. She just says what a lot of kids feel.

Lauren: But what's it got to do with Christmas? I mean . . .
(Song) I Don't See Jesus (see page D)

Lauren:	People making sure they've bought the perfect tree Plastic Santas on the porch for everyone to see.
All 3:	I don't see Jesus in any of these things I don't see the happiness that they're supposed to bring I don't see Jesus in the stores or at the malls I don't see Jesus in any of this at all.
Willie:	Holly wreaths with big red bows hanging on your door Taping wrapping paper till your fingers are so sore.

All 3:   I don't see Jesus in any of these things
I don't see the happiness that they're supposed
    to bring
I don't see Jesus in the stores or at the mall
I don't see Jesus in any of this at all.

Becky: Standing in a line with tired feet and weary knees
And that's just to ask the clerk, "Where's the
    bathroom, please?" *(points to Gracie)*

All 3:   I don't see Jesus in any of these things
I don't feel the happiness that they're supposed
    to bring
I don't see Jesus in the stores or at the mall
I don't see Jesus in any of this at all!

Mr. Anderson: What is it that bothers you the most about Christmas?

Willie: I think it's all the getting. It seems it's all kids care about. I mean, why do we even get gifts at Christmas?

Lauren: What's that got to do with Jesus' birth, anyway?

Mr. Anderson: People long ago wanted to celebrate Christmas by giving a gift to someone they loved. You see, they knew God had given us a wonderful gift, his Son, because he loves us very much. It seemed an appropriate time of the year to show others we love them.

Becky: I get it!

Mr. Anderson: But then something happened over the years. Advertisers realized if they could get people to believe they needed certain things, they would get them at Christmas. Then with television and commercials, advertisers were able to reach one of the best markets of all.

Lauren: Kids!

15

Mr. Anderson: That's right. They knew if kids would ask their parents for it, they'd probably get it.

Willie: So now instead of thinking about what to give someone, we think about what we want to get.

Lauren: And people think buying gifts is the best way to show love.

Becky: Isn't it?

Mr. Anderson: That's not what Jesus taught us. Material things were not important to him. In fact, he warned us how they would get in the way.

Becky: Of what?

Lauren: Of doing God's will.

Willie: Yeah. It's easy to let "things" be important to you. In the end, they don't make you any happier.

Becky: Really?

Lauren: No, Becky. You end up wanting more.

Mr. Anderson: You kids are on the right track. Keep looking for Jesus in Christmas, keep praying for God to help you, and you're going to feel a whole lot better real soon.

Jaime: Hey, Mr. Anderson, let's sing another song! How about "Joy To The World?" *(All the children agree and circle around the piano and sing one verse.)*

Scene II — *(At the mall, Lauren, Becky and Willie are being followed and listened to by Jack.)*

Becky: Look at this wad of money my grandma gave me for Christmas! She said she wanted to buy me a phone like I wanted. I'm glad you two are coming to help me pick it out. It's more fun this way.

Lauren: I have a little to spend, too. The people I babysit for put a few bills in the card they gave to me. How about you, Willie?

Willie: All I have are two quarters my mom gave me to play a video game. She hates those things but said I could play once in a while. Hey, there's one over there. *(They see a video game next to a Salvation Army lady who is ringing a bell.)*

Becky: You mean next to the bell lady?

Lauren: She's collecting for the Salvation Army. They help other people, like the poor, the homeless, you know.

Becky: What a boring way to spend a Saturday afternoon! Waiting for shoppers to be generous.

(They stare at her and she smiles at them. Suddenly, Willie hears "Away In A Manger" — piano softly — as he looks at her.)

Willie: You hear that? *(Music stops)*

Lauren: What? I don't hear anything, do you Becky?

Becky: Just her bell.

Willie: Let's go.

17

Becky: I thought you wanted to play . . .

Willie: Later.

(She wishes them a Merry Christmas as they leave.)

Becky: Wow! She wished us a Merry Christmas even though we didn't give her anything.

Lauren: Yeah. It makes me feel kind of . . .

Willie: Guilty.

Jack: Why should it?

Becky: Rappin' Jack! How long have you been there!

Jack: Consider this your lucky day
    'Cause Rappin' Jack has come your way
    It's being said all over town
    That you kids are really down!

Lauren: We're trying to figure out what's the matter with Christmas.

Willie: It just doesn't feel right.

Jack: Just take a look and open your eyes
    It's everywhere, it's no surprise.
    Tinsel and garland, there's a snow scene
    People are spending all of their green.

Lauren: You tell grownups what they want to hear
    What is it you want for Christmas this year?

Willie: Nintendo and Nikes, tapes and CDs
    Dirt bikes and skateboards with pads for your knees.

Becky: You need a TV, all for your own
And don't forget to get your own phone!

Jack: Now you've got the picture, you'll see that it's fun,
Christmas is the time to think of number one!
(He points to himself)

Willie: Wait! We almost got carried away, like everyone else!
(Willie stomps back to the Salvation Army lady)

Lauren: Willie, wait! What are you doing?

(Willie goes past the video and puts his money in the donation box.)

Becky: He's going crazy, is what he's doing! *(The lady wishes him "Merry Christmas." Lauren walks over and puts her money in the box. The lady speaks to her, too. They look at Becky.)*

Becky: Ah, now wait a minute! This is serious! We're talking a major sacrifice, here. You know how much I want a phone! It's been a lifelong dream of mine! I mean, I deserve it! I've been really good this year! ("Away In The Manger" starts, softly) I did all my homework! I even cleaned under my bed! (Music gets louder) I took Gracie to the bathroom 50 million times! (Louder) I . . . I . . . (Becky looks from her money to the donation box several times. She looks into the smiling face of the woman. Slowly, she drops all her money in. Music stops.)

Lady: God bless you.

Becky: God will, but I'm not sure my grandma will.

Willie: She'll be proud of you.

Lauren: I know we are!

(Jack has been shaking his head in disbelief while watching.)

Jack: I never in my life did see
Kids as crazy as you three.

The inside of your head must be all rocks
To throw all your money into that box!

It goes to people you'll never see
You could have just handed it over to me!

Willie: Come on, Jack! You know you don't need it. And of course we're willing to help people we don't even know. It's what Christians are supposed to do.

Lauren: Let's get going! We're going to be late for practice!

(As they hurry off Jack is totally perplexed, scratches his head and says:)

Jack: Christians! Christians! What peculiar people!
To gather every Sunday under a steeple.

And even worse than that, just as I feared
They want to help others — man, is that weird!

ACT III

(Back at the church. Lauren, Willie and Becky are talking to Mr. Anderson.)

Willie: Then Becky walked up to her and dropped all her money in, too.

Becky: I didn't want to at first. I kept thinking of how badly I wanted my own phone in my room. But then, I remembered what happened with you and Gracie, when you couldn't find Jesus for the nativity.

Mr. Anderson: What do you mean?

Becky: You said you looked before, but you didn't see him because of all the stuff that was in the way. When you got rid of that, you found him. I think that's what's been bothering Willie and Lauren. And I know it's part of what was wrong with me. All of this stuff we think we need to have and do for Christmas can get in the way . . . we can't find Jesus.

Willie: Yeah, Becky, that's it! It felt like it was the right thing to do when we gave our money to that lady. It really felt like . . .

Lauren: Christmas! It's all about giving, not getting, right Mr. Anderson?

Mr. Anderson: You've learned something some grownups never realize. But it doesn't stop at Christmas. We must go right on doing the whole year through what Jesus did when he lived among us. What he calls us to do today.

Willie: We have to give, not take!

Becky: And be servants like he was!

Mr. Anderson: Yes! And Jesus told us when we take care of others, it's the same as if we are taking care of him!

Lauren: And if we don't take care of others, we're turning our backs on Jesus!

(Song) ***God's Greatest Gift*** *(see page E) (Jack is watching from outside.)*

> **Lauren:** God's greatest gift of love came to us at Christmas time
> It was given freely, it didn't cost a dime.

All 3: God came down at Christmas, as Jesus Christ the Son
To show us how we should live, with love for everyone.

Willie: So when we help each other, it's the same as helping him,
Our light of love must shine so bright, we must not let it dim.

All 3: God came down at Christmas, as Jesus Christ the Son
To show us how we all should live, with love for everyone.

Becky: Sometimes it isn't easy and it's very hard to give
We need to pray and read God's Word to show us how to live.

All 3: God came down at Christmas, as Jesus Christ the Son
To show us how we all should live, with love for everyone.

Carol: Hi, Mr. Anderson! The rest of the kids are outside. Can we come in now?

Gracie: I have to go to the bathroom!

Mr. Anderson: Sure! Come in!

Cheryl: Come on in! *(Children start to enter)* We're ready to practice! Everyone gather around the piano. Which song do you want us to sing, Mr. Anderson?

Davey: Let's sing "A Great Big Happy!" *(All children agree.)*

Mr. Anderson: All right, here we go! *(Song) A Great Big Happy (see page C) (Sung by all, Jack comes in and joins.)*

The End

22

A — What's The Matter With Christmas?

P. Futer

Willie:

1. Ev- 'ry one is   in   a hur- ry,   Fran-   tic rush- ing wor-   ry, wor- ry,
2. Ba- king cook- ies   dec- or- a- ting,   look-   ing   at the   bills   and faint- ing,

Lauren:

Driv- ing   to the   mall and shop- ping,   wrap- ping pre- sents   till they're dropping,
Buy- ing   red and   sil-   ver balls,   push- ing, shov- ing   in   the   malls

Becky:

Now   I   know what   I   have missed, I   didn't   put cloth- ing   on   my list!

("What's The Matter With Christmas?" continues on next page)

WHAT'S THE MATTER WITH CHRISTMAS?

Willie: 1. Why is it ev-'ry where we turn At this time of
Lauren: 2. With grown-ups ra-cing all a-round Pull-ing out their

year, There's al-ways one more thing to do As
hair; They're all up tight and some-times yell, Then

Christ-mas time draws near. What's the mat-ter with
kids they think they don't care.

("What's The Matter With Christmas?" continues on next page)

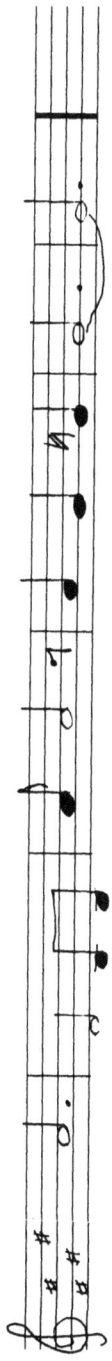

Christ- mas? Is it some- thing I just don't see?

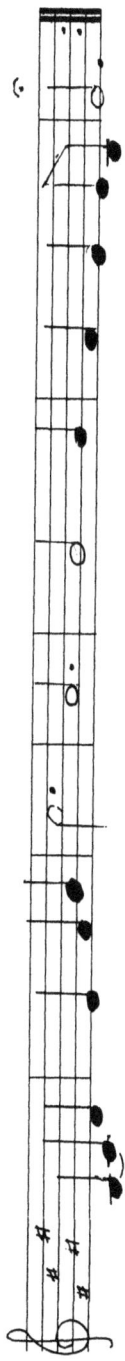

What's the mat- ter with Christ- mas? What's the mat- ter with me?

B — It's Clear To Me

P. Futer

Becky: Snappy

I don't see a prob-lem here,   Things to me are ve-ry clear,

Christ-mas is a won-der-ful time,   Full of gifts most-ly mine!

("It's Clear To Me" continues on next page)

IT'S CLEAR TO ME

I like gum-drops can-dy canes, Get-ting gifts ex-chang-ing names,

It makes me hap-py, can't they see? God would want this all for me!

(spoken)
Wouldn't He?

C — A Great Big Happy

Futer / Gernert

1. Long a- go in Beth- le- hem, Jes- us Christ was born.
2. An- gels start- ed song of praise, they were so filled with joy. They
3. Shep- herds ran to see the ba- by walk- ing was too slow.

1. It was such a hap- py time That first Christ- mas morn.
2. Could not keep the good news quiet a- bout this lit- tle boy. 3. The
3. Ma- ry's face was one big smile She loved her Je- sus so.

("A Great Big Happy" continues on next page)

God felt a great, big hap- py, Too much to keep in- side.

God felt a great, big hap- py, A love He could not hide.

D — I Don't See Jesus

Futer / Gernert

Lauren: Peo- ple mak- ing sure they bought the one per- fect tree;
Willie: Ho-lly wreaths with big, red bows, hang- ing on the door;
Becky: Standing in a line with ti- red feet and weary knees;

Lauren: Plastic San- tas on the porch for ev- 'ry one to see.
Willie: Ta- ping wrap-ping pa- per 'till your fin- gers are so sore!
Becky: And that's just to ask the clerk, "Where's the bathroom please?"

("I Don't See Jesus" continues on next page)

I don't see Jesus in an- y of these things,

I don't feel the hap- pi- ness that they're sup- posed to bring;

I don't see Je- sus in the stores or in the mall,

I don't see Je- sus in an- y of this at all.

E — God's Greatest Gift

Futer / Gernert

Lauren:

, God's great-est gift of love came to us at Christmas time,

It was given free-ly, it did-n't cost a dime

All: Chorus

God came down at Christ-mas as Jes-us Christ, the Son

To show us how we all should live, with love for ev 'ry one

("God's Greatest Gift" continues on next page)

Willie:

So when we help each oth- er It's the same as help- ing Him,

Our light of love must shine so bright, we must not let it dim.

Becky:

Some- times it isn- 't ea- sy and it's ve- ry hard to give,

We need to pray and read God's Word to show us how to live

("God's Greatest Gift" continues on next page)

GOD'S GREATEST GIFT

All: Chorus

God came down at Christ- mas as Je- sus Christ the Son

To show us how we all should live with love for ev 'ry one.